Discover Wheat
and Other Grains™

Refreshing Collection of Recipes

A Simple Approach to Using Whole Grains
Tasty nutrition for any budget

Cary Ruggles

Ruggles Family Productions
Mendon, Utah

Dear Mada:
Happy 80th — *Have a*
great year.

Love Ya
Lela.

ISBN 978-0-615-26545-2

For group presentations please contact us on our website.
www.DiscoverWheat.com

Printed in the United States of America

Second Printing, 2009

Acknowledgments

This good earth provides us with an incredible variety of foods to choose from and enjoy. I am very grateful for a loving Heavenly Father who has provided us with such an abundance and for his help in making this book possible! There are also many family members and others who have helped to shape this work, it has truly become a combined effort.

My wife Patsy has played a significant role in my journey with whole grains, including the development of recipes and the content of this book. She is the one who taught me gratitude and I am truly grateful for her!

The design and overall look of this book is primarily due to two people: my son Joshua Ruggles and my sister Lisa Wheat. Another son, Brandon Ruggles and his wife Sheena have helped to simplify and organize the information so that it is easier to understand. My family's willingness to share their time, talents, and insights to help improve this work is appreciated very much.

Early on, Sherrie Mehl, a cousin, was willing to compare notes on cooking and using wheat, which was very helpful to this effort. In addition, there are many who have been encouraging and supportive along the way by being willing to try samples and discuss the benefits of eating whole grains. Finally, to Richard and Cristal Gordon, good friends, who took the time to proof read this book and share their insights and wisdom, thank you!

"All things which come of the earth, in the season thereof, are made for the benefit and the use of man, both to please the eye and to gladden the heart; yea, for food and for raiment, for taste and for smell, to strengthen the body and to enliven the soul."

(Doctrine & Covenants 59:18, 19)

PREFACE

This is my first effort at writing a book. It was not something that was anticipated, however, I felt a need to share some of the things I have learned about grains. The hope is that this information will help you see how easy it is to include whole grains and other good foods in your diet. In addition to being easy, using whole grains can improve your health, reduce your food budget, help you cope with challenging economic times, and plan for the future. Included in this book is a collection of whole grain recipes along with additional information which should be helpful to those who would like to know more.

It is generally understood that there are significant health benefits associated with a diet made up primarily of fresh fruits and vegetables, legumes, and whole grains. Fruits, vegetables, and legumes are relatively plentiful and easy to use for those individuals who choose to include them in their diet. Although whole grains are also plentiful, they are perceived by many to be difficult to use. Often when people think of using whole grains they envision wheat grinders and baking bread. As good as fresh baked whole wheat bread is, the realities of grinding wheat and making bread seem to prevent many from eating whole grains.

There is a much simpler way to include whole grains in our diets! By cooking the actual grain kernels (berries) like rice is typically cooked, whole grains can be used and enjoyed by everyone. It is amazing how good they are and what can be done with them. An incredible variety of tasty dishes can be created using cooked grain kernels as a base and adding other ingredients such as fruits, vegetables, nuts, and legumes. Experience and enjoy the possibilities whole grains offer with the recipes included in this book!

Thank you for your interest—Bon Appetite!

Cary Ruggles

CONTENTS

INTRODUCTION

Discovering wheat and other grains has been an incredible and unexpected journey! A journey that has only just begun; it will be interesting to see where it leads. To think that whole grains could taste so good was difficult to imagine! This small book is a work in progress. It is the first written attempt to share my experience using grains with others; something I have felt a need to do. Although not an expert on wheat or other grains, I am a dedicated student continually learning about nutrition and health. The effect that nutrition has on our health and our bodies is truly amazing. Due to a change of diet and eating more healthy foods, my health and life have improved dramatically. The human body is a very miraculous and complex system that functions best when we treat it as the temple that it is, and give it what it needs.

My experience with wheat and other grains began in March of 2008. Looking for ways to reduce our food budget and also trying to figure out how to use existing food storage (primarily wheat that was over 30 years old), I decided to start eating wheat. The quest began by looking for ways to prepare it. Initially, thoughts of whole wheat bread and cracked wheat cereal came to mind, which were familiar methods of using wheat. However, grinding wheat and baking bread was time consuming and just eating cracked wheat cereal seemed like it would get old quickly. Therefore, the search for wheat-based recipes began.

In an old recipe book there was a recipe entitled, "Prairie Wheat Cereal". The recipe simply called for soaking and cooking the whole kernels of wheat (also referred to as wheat berries) in water and serving it with honey and nuts as a cooked cereal. That recipe became the starting point and helped me to focus on eating whole grain kernels. Almost all of the wheat and other grains my wife and I have been preparing and eating have been cooked as whole grain kernels, not ground in a wheat grinder.

Using Whole Grains

It is interesting to note that although the United States is primarily a wheat-eating country, the vast majority of the wheat consumed by its citizens has been ground and processed into white flour. This is a trend which began with a milling invention that made it possible to "refine" flour by separating and removing the bran and germ from the grain. Very little of the wheat and other grains eaten in the United States are in the whole grain kernel form (other than rice). In many ways it seems that we are missing out on much of the enjoyment and benefits whole grains have to offer us.

Whole Grains & Whole Grain Kernels

There are five common methods for using whole grains, which are: ground into flour, cracked, flaked (rolled), sprouted, and used as whole kernels (berries). In addition, there is another way to prepare grains, that I refer to as "creamed". By cooking the whole grain kernels with more water and for a longer period of time, the berries (kernels) can then be creamed, creating a wonderful way to prepare and eat whole grains. In addition to creaming wheat berries, other whole grains can also be creamed and used in various recipes.

The term "whole grain" can refer to either whole kernels of grain, cracked grain, rolled grain, or grain ground into flour as long as all of the parts of the kernel (which include the bran, endosperm, and germ) are used. In fact "whole grain" is a defined term in the food industry. Typically, it denotes grain kernels that have been ground into flour and used in commercial products.

There does not seem to be a specific term or phrase that describes using whole kernels of grain which have not been altered or processed in any way. Although some grains (such as oats) are known as groats if they have been hulled and the grain kernel is intact with the bran. In this book, the terms "whole grain kernels" or "whole grain berries" (or similar terms which include "kernels" or "berries") are used to refer to whole kernels of grain that are still intact.

Overcoming Barriers to Using Whole Grains

The primary focus of this book is to share ways to prepare and serve whole grain kernels, both as whole berries and creamed. As enjoyable as whole grains ground into flour, cracked, or sprouted are, these methods of using grain seem to create a number of barriers to using whole grains for many people. Some of the barriers that prevent individuals from eating and enjoying whole grains include: a lack of equipment (such as a wheat grinder), time, experience, and knowledge; feeling overwhelmed or a dislike for some whole grain products. I have also struggled with a number of these barriers!

Using grains in the whole kernel form can virtually eliminate the barriers to using whole grains. No special equipment or experience is required, they are easy to prepare, and grain berry recipes taste great! In addition, there is nothing to fear because <u>you can begin right now</u>, with what you already have, so there is no reason to feel overwhelmed. You can join the growing number of people enjoying the benefits of eating whole grains.

When I initially decided to eat wheat, it was done with mixed feelings. The thought of saving money on our food budget and figuring out how to use stored wheat was exciting, however, it seemed that eating a lot of wheat could be somewhat unpleasant. It did not take long to realize that my concern was unfounded. The anticipated drudgery turned out to be a <u>real joy</u>. The wheat tasted great and using the whole grain wheat like rice made cooking and preparing wheat and other grains much easier.

Whole grain kernels used in recipes are surprisingly delicious, and the ease of cooking whole grains on the stove or in a crock pot is very similar to preparing other types of meals. In addition, the health and financial benefits of eating whole grains combined with other good foods can be substantial. The world is changing and economic pressures have increased rapidly. Whether it is to reduce short-term food expenditures or to store for the future, whole grains are a good choice. Discovering and enjoying cooked whole grain kernels has been like finding an incredible hidden treasure! Hopefully, it will be a treasure for you as well.

CREATING THE RECIPES

Shortly after beginning to cook and eat whole grain wheat berries, I started searching for ways to improve the variety and enjoyment of the wheat I was eating. The search led my wife and I to the kitchen to create a number of tasty whole grain recipes. When we discovered how good grain berries can be, we were amazed that using grains (such as wheat) in the whole kernel form is not more common—it was like finding a whole new food group. Properly prepared, whole grain kernels taste great and are a wonderful addition to anyone's diet. The nutritional benefits are an added plus that confirm that whole grains are an incredible food source.

In addition, wheat and many of the other common grains will keep very well (for about one week) when refrigerated. Our method of preparing and storing grains has, in effect, made whole grains a "healthy fast food"! Grains can be cooked in large batches once a week, used in various recipes and stored to be used as needed throughout the week. With a little advance preparation, healthy eating can also be convenient. Likewise, there are ways to speed up the cooking and preparation process which will be shared later in this book.

Food is one of life's pleasures that is meant to be enjoyed! Based on the incredible variety of fruits, vegetables, and grains, etc. that have been created for our use, it is apparent that our Creator wanted us to enjoy the foods that sustain our lives. The range of shapes, colors, and tastes of the foods we eat are spectacular, they are as much a feast for the eyes as they are for the palate. Fresh fruits and vegetables have always been very enjoyable to me. However, it was a real surprise that whole grains taste so good—which was a very welcome discovery. The recipes in this book were created to complement the flavors, textures, and colors that nature has provided for us to enjoy.

Developing the recipes was a process of cooking the whole grain kernels and then adding various other ingredients such as fruits, vegetables, legumes, nuts, honey, spices, and seasonings. About anything can be added to cooked whole grain berries and it will taste good as long as the ingredients used have complementary flavors. In addition to whole grain based recipes, like those in this book, grain berries can be added to existing recipes or meals. For example cooked grain berries can be substituted for rice in recipes that include rice as an ingredient. It is amazing how many ways there are to enjoy whole grains. Once you start looking, opportunities to use them are everywhere!

The recipes in this book are divided in to two sections: "Cooking Grain Berries" and "Grain Berry Recipes". Because cooked whole grains will keep so well, the whole grain kernels can be cooked (without other ingredients) in large batches and stored in the refrigerator to be used in recipes as needed. The recipes for cooking basic whole grains are in the Cooking Grain Berries section, whereas, the Grain Berry Recipes section focuses on creating finished dishes by combining cooked grain berries with other ingredients.

Although most of the recipes in this book specify Wheat Berries, virtually any type of cooked whole grain kernels can be substituted for the wheat. Multi-grain recipes have been included along with the wheat berry recipes in the Cooking Grain Berries section. It is actually difficult to tell the difference between the taste of wheat and the multi-grain mix when combined with other ingredients. Whether you use Wheat Berries, the multi-grain mix, or other grains, enjoy the recipes and have fun trying new things with whole grains!

NUTRITION & HEALTH

Research confirms that there are a number of potential health benefits associated with eating whole grains. The International Food Information Council ("IFIC"), citing many studies, states on its website (10/23/08), "Whole grains contain many healthful components, including dietary fiber, starch, essential fatty acids, antioxidants, vitamins, minerals, lignans, and phenolic compounds, that have been linked to reduced risk of heart disease, cancer, diabetes, obesity, and other chronic diseases. Since most of the health-promoting components are found in the [grain] germ and bran, foods made with whole grains can play an important role in maintaining good health."

Quoting from the Iowa Women's Health Study (American Journal of Clinical Nutrition), the IFIC further addresses the significance of the grain kernel, "The health advantages to whole grains are largely associated with consuming the whole grain 'package', which includes vitamins, minerals, essential fatty acids, phytochemicals and other bioactive food components." The Whole Grains Council, on its website (10/25/08), identifies the following health benefits of using whole grains, based on repeated studies as a: "reduced risk of stroke, type 2 diabetes, heart disease, and better weight maintenance." It further outlines other health benefits indicated by recent studies which include a: "reduced risk of asthma, healthier carotid arteries, [reduced risk] of inflammatory disease, lower risk of colorectal cancer, healthier blood pressure levels, and less gum disease and tooth loss." The list of potential benefits goes on!

Benefits of a Natural Diet

Interestingly, in the second edition of his book entitled, The Word of Wisdom, John A. Widtsoe (a Latter-day Saint Apostle [1921-1952] and avid student of nutrition), documented a stark contrast between the diets and diseases of what he called "civilized people" and "nature people" (groups of people isolated from civilization). Degenerative diseases in the United States of America (a "civilized people") rose significantly from 1900 to 1946 (pages 4 & 5) (a trend that has unfortunately continued to our day), whereas, degenerative diseases were practically unknown to the "nature people". The diet of the "nature people" consisted of "unmilled grains, fruits, and vegetables, with a [limited] amount of goat's milk, butter, and meat…." As noted by Widtsoe, it was "just such a diet as outlined in the Word of Wisdom" (pages 228 and 229).

Similarly, Dr. Ray D. Strand, a medical doctor and nutritional specialist, under the heading, "Healthy Lifestyle" on his website, stated, "An increased amount of fiber is very important in our overall diet and can be found in fruits, vegetables, and whole grains." He then went on to share the experience of Dr. Denis Burkitt, a practicing surgeon in Africa for 20 years, known for his discovery of "Burkitt's Lymphoma". "While in Africa, [Dr. Burkitt] did not see a single case of colon cancer, diverticulitis, hemorrhoids, gall bladder disease, or appendicitis among the native population. He attributed this remarkable finding to the fact that his native African patients consumed 60 to 70 grams of fiber per day . . . ." Upon returning to the United States, Dr Burkitt devoted "most of his time promoting the health benefits of a high fiber diet."

Variety & Nutrition

From my personal experience of eating a significant amount of cooked whole grains combined with various fruits and vegetables, I too can see the wisdom of a balanced diet consisting primarily of fresh fruits, vegetables, and whole grains. Variety is also an essential component of a healthy diet, both from the actual nutrients received, as well as, the enjoyment and satisfaction experienced. According to Widtsoe, it "is well known [that] food which appeals to [and stimulates] the senses becomes more appetizing and thus actually aids digestion" (page 124).

Each of the foods we eat is made up of different types and amounts of proteins, carbohydrates, fats, minerals, vitamins, water, and other nutrients. When a variety of foods are eaten within each of the different food groups, whether it be grains, fruits, vegetables, etc., we receive a more complete range of the different nutrients our bodies need to function properly. Although initially we ate wheat berries exclusively, we now typically use a multi-grain mix (which is made up of 50 percent wheat). This basic multi-grain recipe is included in this book.

Adding Whole Grains to Your Diet

For those of you who would like to add whole grains to your diet, experts in the field suggest that you add them gradually to help your body and digestive system adjust to the healthy change. Eating whole grain kernels is very different from the typical American diet. You can begin by eating a small quantity of one type of grain (such as wheat) in one of the recipes included in this book, and then increase the serving size a little each day until you reach your desired amount. Another approach is to replace some of the rice in familiar recipes with an equivalent amount of cooked whole grain kernels, and then gradually increase the amount of grain kernels. However you chose to do it, just get started!

While most individuals should adjust very well to adding whole grains to their diet, some may be intolerant to or have an allergic reaction to whole wheat or other grains. If this is the case for you, one option is to identify the grain(s) causing the problem and reduce or eliminate those grain(s) from your diet. If wheat is identified as the cause, another option is to replace wheat with other grains which are gluten free, or spelt (a grain that is very similar to wheat) which can be tolerated much better by some than wheat. Certainly, from the perspective of storing grains for future use (especially in a time of significant need) it would be best to determine in advance which of the grains work best for you and your family.

Daniel Eats Pulse

An interesting insight is gained into the benefit of whole grains from the Old Testament in the Bible. Recorded in the book of Daniel, is an experience that Daniel, Hananiah, Mishael, and Azariah had in the king's court. After Nebuchadnezzar of Babylon conquered Jerusalem around 605 B.C., Daniel and his brethren, who were members of Judah's upper class, were captured and carried to Babylon to serve in the king's court. There they were taught the ways of the Babylonians.

While serving in the king's court, captives typically ate the "king's meat" (food and wine from the king's table), however, Daniel and his brethren refused to eat the "kings meat" or drink his wine. This was done to remain true to the Lord by not eating food inconsistent with the requirements of Jewish law. Therefore, Daniel proposed a 10 day test, wherein he and his brethren would eat "pulse" and drink water instead of eating and drinking from the kings table. Following which, they would then be compared to the other captives in the kings court.

The prince of the eunuchs agreed and after the 10 days the two different groups of young men were compared with each other. The health of Daniel's group, which had been eating pulse, proved to be much better than that of the other captives who had been eating the "king's meat" and drinking his wine. According to the Bible Dictionary, in Hebrew the "word [pulse] denotes seeds", and in the Latter-day Saint Institute Old Testament Student Manual it states, " Pulse is such seeds and grains as peas, wheat, barley, and rye." A version of Daniel's pulse has been included with the recipes in this book. Daniel and his brethren experienced significant benefits from eating whole grains and so can we!

Word of Wisdom Insights

The 89th section of the <u>Doctrine and Covenants</u> (a Latter-day Saint volume of scripture) sets forth the Lord's code of health through divine revelation. Commonly referred to as the "Word of Wisdom", the 89th section focuses primarily on ways to improve human health through proper nutrition. Although a lot of attention is focused on avoiding harmful substances, the real gems in the Word of Wisdom are the things we are admonished <u>to use</u> that will help to ensure good health. It seems clear from this inspired document, that the majority of our diet should be made up of edible fruits and vegetables and various types of grains. In the 89th section, we are counseled by the Lord:

- To use all wholesome herbs and fruits as food (whether in the ground or above the ground) in the season thereof with prudence and thanksgiving (compiled from verses 10, 11, and 16).

- That all grain is ordained for the use of man and of beasts, to be the staff of life; that all grain is good for the food of man, nevertheless, wheat is for man; and that barley and other grains are for mild drinks (compiled from verses 14, 16, and 17).

A careful study of the Word of Wisdom, makes it clear that grain (primarily wheat) should play a significant role in our overall diet. However, some ways of eating grains are more healthy than others. Highly processed grain, such as bleached white flour, is a very prevalent ingredient in the food supply of most advanced societies. An increasing body of evidence suggests that this is not a healthy trend. In fact, highly processed white flour has been implicated as a significant contributor to the rapid increase of degenerative diseases in developed countries, with the United States leading the way.

Although the market is flooded with unhealthy food options containing some "form of grain" (primarily white flour), unprocessed grains are still readily available. In the past my wife and I have not used grains very much. Like many, we did not really know how to use them, however, that has changed. Learning how to prepare and use whole grain kernels has been an incredible discovery for us! As mentioned before it was like finding a whole new food group. Now our fridge is always packed with pre-cooked grains and various ready-to-eat grain dishes—our "healthy fast food". Since whole grains have become a significant part of our diet, I have truly gained a great appreciation for the Lord's revealed truths in the 89th section, regarding the importance of eating grains!

<u>Word of Wisdom Promises</u>:

The Lord concludes the 89th section of the <u>Doctrine and Covenants</u> with some significant promises, which are found in the last four verses. Those who adhere to the tenets of the Word of Wisdom and are obedient to the commandments are promised that they: "shall receive health in their navel and marrow in their bones; and shall find wisdom and great treasures of knowledge, even hidden treasures; and shall run and not be weary and shall walk and not faint." Further, the Lord promises, "that the destroying angel shall pass by them … and not slay them" (found in verses 18-21).

In his book, The Word of Wisdom, John A. Widtsoe stated, "The many 'do's' in the inspired document are as important as the 'don'ts'." Widtsoe went on to explain that people who are faithful to the Lord's code of health, "would receive a greater fullness of the promised reward—a long life of physical health, while the destroying angel of sickness and death would pass by and not slay them" (Page 12).

Widtsoe's insights helped me see the Lord's promises in a different light. In the past, I have envisioned the destroying angel referred to in verse 21 somewhat abstractly, not as a direct consequence of poor dietary choices. The good news, however, is that wise nutritional choices can help us realize a long life in good physical health! The following sections will show you how to cook whole grain kernels and tasty nutritious ways to use them.

COOKING METHODS

There are a number of different ways to cook whole grain kernels. Three are covered in this book (in the Cooking Grain Berries recipe section): a conventional pan on a stove, a slow cooker (crock pot), and a pressure cooker. The primary differences in the cooking methods is the type of equipment and the required cooking times. Use the method that is best for you, they all work very well. The easiest and cheapest way to get started is to use what you already have. Because cooking with a pressure cooker may be new to some, information has been included about them in this section.

Pressure Cooker Overview

About a month after beginning to cook and eat whole wheat berries, I began looking for a pressure cooker to cook them in. My cousin had also started cooking wheat and had reduced her cooking time significantly using a pressure cooker. The thought of cooking wheat kernels quicker was very intriguing. After researching pressure cookers in general and then comparing specific brands, it became apparent that pressure cookers have improved significantly over the years, especially from a safety perspective.

Based on the research, we chose a "Kuhn Rikon" pressure cooker, which was highly recommended for quality, durability, and performance. It wasn't the cheapest brand available, but it works very well and gets used a lot. One of the features that is especially attractive is the built in "5-way safety system" to help ensure safe, trouble-free operation. Another option that was considered was an electric pressure cooker that sits on the counter similar to a rice cooker. They are easy to use and turn off automatically when done. Typically they have settings for both time and pressure. While electric pressure cookers are very convenient, they may not be as durable as a good quality stove top model.

In addition to being quicker, pressure cookers are cheaper to operate than other methods of cooking grains because they use less energy. They also work great on other foods, as well as, whole grains. It is claimed, that foods (such as vegetables) cooked in them taste better and are healthier due to a reduced cooking time. Another nice thing about pressure cookers is that they typically cook very consistently. If you are considering buying or using a pressure cooker, it would be wise to understand its recommended capacities in advance. Often there are limits on how full they should be filled (see manufacturer's recommendations).

Cooking Grains With a Pressure Cooker

A pressure cooker can be a great tool when used properly. Pressure cooker companies often recommend <u>not</u> cooking cereal grains in the actual pot. Cereal grains (such as wheat) expand as they cook and are typically very frothy, which can obstruct and/or interfere with pressure relief valves, which can compromise safety. However, whole grains can be cooked in a separate covered pot on a trivet inside a pressure cooker (using it as a double boiler), as recommended by one manufacturer. The following guidelines are provided to show a method for cooking whole grain kernels in a pressure cooker. <u>To ensure safe operation</u>, follow the manufacture's recommendations!

<u>Pressure Cooker Guidelines:</u>

- An inner pot (ours is a stainless steel bain marie) is used to place the grain kernels and other ingredients in, instead of the actual pressure cooker pot, creating in effect a "double boiler".
- The inner pot is covered with foil and crimped around the rim to seal it.
- To prevent the inner pot from contacting the bottom of the pressure cooker, a trivet is placed inside the pressure cooker on the bottom.
- The bottom of the inner pot must be sitting in water for it to work as a double boiler. The water should be about 2 1/2" deep (when the inner pot is sitting on the trivet).
- The pressure cooker lid is then put on and secured to begin cooking.
- Using this method, whole grains can be cooked at a high pressure level (15 pounds), which will reduce the cooking time.
- The pressure should <u>always</u> be released before opening a pressure cooker, there are multiple way s to release the pressure, some of which may be dependent on the type of pressure cooker (see instruction manual for manufacturer's recommendations).

STORING COOKED GRAINS

Cooked grain berries and creamy grain berries keep very well in a refrigerator for about one week. However, once combined in a recipe with other ingredients, the ingredient with the shortest storage life will likely determine the overall time that a dish will keep. Refrigerated creamy grain berries will set up and look somewhat like condensed soup. To restore the creamy grain berry texture (which is typically like a creamy sauce that is not too watery) simply mix with water.

Most cooked grains can also be frozen and stored for longer periods of time. Frozen creamy grain berries may have a tendency to separate a little when thawed. A good way to restore the creamy texture after freezing is to add water and stir thoroughly while reheating.

COOKING GRAIN BERRIES

The following basic recipes for Wheat Berries and Creamy Wheat Berries are used in other recipes throughout this book. Both can be cooked in advance in large batches and combined later in recipes with other ingredients because they keep so well when refrigerated. To help make cooking whole grain kernels easy, regardless of equipment or skills, multiple basic recipes have been included. There are three separate recipes for cooking basic Wheat Berries, each of which outlines a different method for cooking the grain. Similarly, there are also three recipes for cooking Creamy Wheat Berries. In addition, a multi-grain recipe is included with each of the basic wheat berry recipes.

Now it is time to jump in and get started! It is easy to do and you will be surprised how good whole grains can taste. There can be variables with anything you cook, including grain, so it may be necessary to adjust cooking times to compensate for differences in appliances, elevation, etc. The important thing is to get started and cook the grain the way you like it!

Wheat Berries
Yield ~ 12 cups
Estimated Preparation Time ~ 1 hour 10 minutes

(Wheat Berries are used as a basic ingredient for other recipes in this book)

- 4 cups ~ Wheat kernels
- 8 cups ~ Water
- 1 tsp. ~ Salt

---

1. Place grain, water, and salt in a large pan (5 quarts or more) and stir.
2. Bring mixture to a boil over high heat.
3. Reduce heat, place lid on pan and simmer (just below boiling) until done ~ about 1 hour 5 minutes.
    - Kernels should be chewy with some kernels broken open when done.
    - Mixture should always be wet while cooking.
4. Drain any remaining water.
5. Use or store in a refrigerator.

ଓ Ideally, little or no water should be left over after cooking the grain, however, until you know how it cooks on your stove it may be best to begin by using a little extra water.

Multi-Grain Berries
Follow the Wheat Berries recipe above with the following changes:
1. Replace wheat kernels with the grains listed below.
    - 2 cups ~ Wheat kernels
    - 2/3 cup ~ Barley kernels (hulled)
    - 2/3 cup ~ Oat kernels (groats)
    - 2/3 cup ~ Rye kernels
2. Reduce simmering time by about 5 minutes.

ଓ Multi-Grain Berries can be substituted for Wheat Berries in other recipes.

ଓ Using multiple grains adds variety and nutrients.

Creamy Wheat Berries
Yield ~ 12 cups
Estimated Preparation Time ~ 2 hours 20 minutes

(Creamy Wheat Berries are used as a basic ingredient for other recipes in this book)

- 3 cups - Wheat kernels
- 13 1/2 cups - Water
- 3/4 tsp. - Salt
- Water for mixing ~ about 3 cups

---

1. Place grain, water, and salt in a large pan (6 quarts or more) and stir.
2. Bring mixture to a boil over high heat.
3. Reduce heat, place lid on pan and simmer (just below boiling) until done (mixture should be soft and soupy) ~ about 2 hours 10 minutes.
4. Scoop soft kernels into a large mixing bowl.
5. Mix until thick and creamy with hand mixer (on high speed) ~ about 2 -3 min.
6. Add water for mixing as needed and mix to desired creamy texture.
    - The texture should be like a creamy sauce that is not too watery.
7. Use or store in a refrigerator.

❧ When the grain is cooked completely:
    - Kernels should be very soft and many should be broken open.
    - Ideally, water should not be visible on top of the cooked grain.

Creamy Multi-Grain Berries
Follow the Creamy Wheat Berries recipe above with the following changes:

1. Replace wheat kernels with the grains listed below.
    - 1 1/2 cups - Wheat kernels
    - 1/2 cup - Barley kernels (hulled)
    - 1/2 cup - Oat kernels (groats)
    - 1/2 cup - Rye kernels
2. Reduce simmering time by about 10 minutes.

❧ Creamy Multi-Grain Berries can be substituted for Creamy Wheat Berries in other recipes.
❧ Using multiple grains adds variety and nutrients.

Wheat Berries
Yield ~ 12 cups

Estimated Preparation Time ~ 2 to 3 hours

(Wheat Berries are used as a basic ingredient for other recipes in this book)

- 4 cups ~ Wheat kernels
- 1 tsp. ~ Salt
- 7 cups ~ Water

---

1. Place grain, water, and salt in a slow cooker (Crock Pot) and stir.
2. Cook until done ~ <u>about 2 to 3 hours</u> (slow cooker temperatures may vary).
   - Kernels should be chewy with some kernels broken open when done.
   - Mixture should always be wet while cooking.
3. Drain any remaining water.
4. Use or store in a refrigerator.

❥ Ideally, little or no water should be left over after cooking the grain, however, until you know how it cooks in your slow cooker (Crock Pot) it may be best to begin by using a little extra water.

Multi-Grain Berries

Follow the Wheat Berries recipe above with the following changes:

1. Replace wheat kernels with the grains listed below.
   - 2 cups ~ Wheat kernels
   - 2/3 cup ~ Oat kernels (groats)
   - 2/3 cup ~ Barley kernels (hulled)
   - 2/3 cup ~ Rye kernels
2. Reduce cooking time by <u>about 15 minutes</u>.

❥ Multi-Grain Berries can be substituted for Wheat Berries in other recipes.

❥ Using multiple grains adds variety and nutrients.

Creamy Wheat Berries
Yield ~ 12 cups
Estimated Preparation Time ~ 4 to 5 hours

(Creamy Wheat Berries are used as a basic ingredient for other recipes in this book)

- 3 cups ~ Wheat kernels
- 12 cups ~ Water
- 3/4 tsp. ~ Salt
- Water for mixing ~ about 2 cups

1. Place grain, water, and salt in a slow cooker (Crock Pot) and stir.
2. Cook until done (mixture should be soft and soupy) ~ <u>about 4 to 5 hours</u> (slow cooker temperatures may vary).
3. Scoop soft kernels into a large mixing bowl.
4. Mix until thick and creamy with hand mixer (on high speed) ~ <u>about 2 ~3 min.</u>
5. Add water for mixing as needed and mix to desired creamy texture.
    - The texture should be like a creamy sauce that is not too watery.
6. Use or store in a refrigerator.

℞ When the grain is cooked completely:
    - Kernels should be very soft and many should be broken open.
    - Ideally, water should not be visible on top of the cooked grain.

Creamy Multi-Grain Berries

Follow the Creamy Wheat Berries recipe above with the following changes:

1. Replace wheat kernels with the grains listed below.
   - 1 1/2 cups ~ Wheat kernels
   - 1/2 cup ~ Barley kernels (hulled)
   - 1/2 cup ~ Oat kernels (groats)
   - 1/2 cup ~ Rye kernels
2. Reduce cooking time by <u>about 25 minutes</u>.

℞ Creamy Multi-Grain Berries can be substituted for Creamy Wheat Berries in other recipes.

℞ Using multiple grains adds variety and nutrients.

Wheat Berries

Yield ~ 12 cups

Estimated Preparation Time ~ 40 minutes

(Wheat Berries are used as a basic ingredient for other recipes in this book)

- 4 cups ~ Wheat kernels
- 6 2/3 cups ~ Water
- 1 tsp. ~ Salt

For more information about the Pressure Cooker Method refer to the "Cooking Grains With a Pressure Cooker" section (page 14).

1. Place grain, water, and salt in the inner pot and stir.
2. Cover inner pot with aluminum foil (tightly) and crimp around rim to seal.
3. Place inner pot in the pressure cooker on a trivet in water that is about 2 1/2" deep (when the inner pot is sitting on the trivet) and secure the lid.
4. Cook on high heat until the high pressure level (15 pounds) is reached.
5. Reduce heat as needed to maintain high pressure level.
6. Cook at high pressure for ~ about 25 minutes.
7. Remove from heat and let sit until pressure is released completely.
   - Kernels should be chewy with some kernels broken open when done.
8. Drain any remaining water.
9. Use or store in a refrigerator.

᎒ Ideally, little or no water should be left over after cooking the grain, however, until you know how it cooks in your pressure cooker it may be best to begin by using a little extra water.

Multi-Grain Berries

Follow the Wheat Berries recipe above with the following changes:
1. Replace wheat kernels with the grains listed below.
   - 2 cups ~ Wheat kernels
   - 2/3 cup ~ Barley kernels (hulled)
   - 2/3 cup ~ Oat kernels (groats)
   - 2/3 cup ~ Rye kernels
2. Reduce cooking time by about 2 minutes.

᎒ Multi-Grain Berries can be substituted for Wheat Berries in other recipes.

᎒ Using multiple grains adds variety and nutrients.

Creamy Wheat Berries

Yield ~ 12 cups

Estimated Preparation Time ~ 1 hour 10 minutes

(Creamy Wheat Berries are used as a basic ingredient for other recipes in this book).

- 3 cups ~ Wheat kernels
- 7 1/2 cups ~ Water
- 3/4 tsp. ~ Salt
- Water for mixing ~ about 3 cups

For more information about the Pressure Cooker Method refer to the "Cooking Grains With a Pressure Cooker" section (page 14).

1. Place grain, water, and salt in the inner pot and stir.
2. Cover inner pot with aluminum foil (tightly) and crimp around rim to seal.
3. Place inner pot in the pressure cooker on a trivet in water that is about 2 1/2" deep (when the inner pot is sitting on the trivet) and secure the lid.
4. Cook on high heat until the high pressure level (15 pounds) is reached.
5. Reduce heat as needed to maintain high pressure level.
6. Cook at high pressure for ~ about 50 minutes.
7. Remove from heat and let sit until pressure is released completely.
8. Scoop soft kernels into a large mixing bowl (mixture should be soft and soupy).
9. Mix until thick and creamy with hand mixer (on high speed) ~ about 2 ~3 min.
10. Add water for mixing as needed and mix to desired creamy texture.
    - The texture should like a creamy sauce that is not too watery.
11. Use or store in a refrigerator.

ᗇ When the grain is cooked completely:
   - Kernels should be very soft and many should be broken open.
   - Ideally, water should not be visible on top of the cooked grain.

Creamy Multi-Grain Berries

Follow the Creamy Wheat Berries recipe above with the following changes:
1. Replace wheat kernels with the grains listed below.
    - 1 1/2 cups ~ Wheat kernels
    - 1/2 cup ~ Barley kernels (hulled)
    - 1/2 cup ~ Oat kernels (groats)
    - 1/2 cup ~ Rye kernels
2. Reduce simmering time by about 5 minutes.

ᗇ Creamy Multi-Grain Berries can be substituted for Creamy Wheat Berries in other recipes.

ᗇ Using multiple grains adds variety and nutrients.

GRAIN BERRY RECIPES

As whole grains became a significant part of my diet, my wife and I began creating a collection of recipes using wheat berries combined with other ingredients that have complementary flavors. Initially, the only grain used was wheat, however, with time other grains were added for variety and to improve available nutrients. Now we typically use a multi-grain mix in the following recipes in place of wheat. That multi-grain mix recipe has been included with each of the basic grain recipes in the Cooking Grain Berries section (pages 16-21).

Fresh fruits and vegetables are included in the recipes as much as possible. However, the convenience and variety of frozen fruits and vegetables can make preparing and eating whole grains much simpler. Also, spices and premixed seasonings are used in many of the recipes and should be readily available.

It is amazing how good whole grains can taste if they are prepared well! Good food is a pleasure to be savored. The following recipes have been created to please the palate, hopefully you will enjoy them as we have. Use these recipes as a starting point to help you discover the enjoyment and benefit of making whole grains a regular part of your diet. Then get creative and develop your own—Enjoy!

∙ To help you get started, try some of our favorite recipes that are easy to prepare such as:
- Wheat Berry Porridge (page 23)
- Apple Cinnamon Wheat Berries (page 24)
- Vegetable Wheat Berries (page 33)
- Wheat Berry Stir Fry (page 34)
- Chicken & Wheat Berries (page 36)

Wheat Berry Porridge

Yield ~ 2 1/2 cups

Estimated Preparation Time ~ 5 to 10 minutes

(A great warm breakfast that can be served anytime)

- 2 cups ~ Creamy Wheat Berries
  (precooked ~ pages 17, 19, or 21)
- Water for thinning (if needed)
- 1/4 cup ~ Almonds (whole/sliced)
- 1 ~ 2 Tbsp. ~ Honey
- 1/4 tsp. ~ Vanilla (optional)
- Fresh or dried fruit (as desired)

---

1. Place fresh warm Creamy Wheat Berries in a bowl.
   - If they have been refrigerated or frozen add water (as needed), mix to desired creamy consistency and warm (mix while warming if frozen).
2. Stir in honey, almonds, vanilla, and fruit as desired.
3. Welcome the day with a warm hearty breakfast that will get you going!

ᘓ Wheat Berry Porridge has become one of my favorite breakfast foods!

Suggestions:

- Try eating Wheat Berry Porridge without milk, it is great alone.
- Top with raisins, seeds, or other tasty goodies.
- Experiment with different types of spices and/or flavorings, such as cinnamon or mint, etc.
- Try adding different types of fresh or dried fruit.
- Substitute other nuts for the almonds.
- Replace the Creamy Wheat Berries with Creamy Multi-Grain Berries (pages 17, 19, or 21) for more variety.

ᘓ Most of all, relax and enjoy the soothing taste of a warm bowl of Porridge!

Apple Cinnamon Wheat Berries

Yield ~ 7 cups

Estimated Preparation Time ~ 5 minutes

(Good served for breakfast, a snack, or anytime for a sweet treat)

- 4 cups ~ Wheat Berries (chilled) (precooked ~ pages 16, 18, or 20)
- 2 medium ~ Apples (3/8" cubes)
- 1 cup ~ Almonds (whole or sliced)
- 4 Tbsp. ~ Honey
- 4 tsp. ~ Cinnamon (ground)
- 1 Tbsp. ~ Water

---

1. Cut apples into (3/8" cubes).
2. Mix chilled Wheat Berries, cubed apples, and almonds together in a large bowl.
3. Add honey, cinnamon, and water (as needed) and mix well.
4. Serve cold or warm for a healthy treat!

CB Cinnamon Wheat Berries are a real favorite of many.

CB Kids love this one!

Suggestions:

- Replace the apples and almonds with other fruits and nuts.
- Try different spices/seasonings in place of the cinnamon.
- Top with raisins, seeds, or other tasty goodies.
- Add Apple Cinnamon Wheat Berries to yogurt, pudding, ice cream, and other desserts.
- Sprinkle these chewy morsels on salads to add a little sweetness.
- Enjoy Multi-Grain Berries (pages 16, 18, or 20) with this recipe in place of the Wheat Berries.

Orange Cranberry Wheat Berries
Yield ~ 7 cups
Estimated Preparation Time ~ 10 minutes
(Refreshing breakfast or side dish)

- 4 cups ~ Wheat Berries (chilled)
  (precooked ~ pages 16, 18, or 20)
- 1 1/2 cups ~ Oranges (3/8" bits)
- 3/4 cup ~ Craisins
- 3/4 cup ~ Pine nuts (shelled)
- 5 Tbsp. ~ Honey
- 2 Tbsp. ~ Orange juice

- 1 Tbsp. ~ Flax seeds
- 1 tsp. ~ Cinnamon (ground)
- 1 tsp. ~ Fresh ginger (finely minced)
- 1 tsp. ~ Ginger (ground)
- 1/4 tsp. ~ Cloves (ground)
- 1/4 tsp. ~ Orange peel (grated)

---

1. Cut oranges into (3/8" bits).
2. Mix chilled Wheat Berries, oranges bits, Craisins, and pine nuts together in a large bowl.
3. Blend honey, orange juice, flax seeds, seasonings, and orange peel, in a small mixing bowl.
4. Pour blended mixture over Wheat Berries and other ingredients and mix together well.
5. Serve cold for a tangy treat!

❧ This yummy dish will get your attention!

Suggestions:

- Substitute pine nuts with cooked great northern white beans, they are a very complementary taste.
- Top with seeds or other tasty goodies.
- Experiment with other fruits that have complementary flavors.
- Add Orange Cranberry Wheat Berries to yogurt, pudding, ice cream, and other desserts.
- Sprinkle on salads to liven things up.
- Add a twist to this fun dish by using Multi-Grain Berries (pages 16, 18, or 20) instead of Wheat Berries.

Garden Wheat Berry Salad

Yield ~ 9 1/2 cups

Estimated Preparation Time ~ 15 to 20 minutes (dressing) / 25 minutes (salad)

(Great served as a salad, lettuce wrap, or as a salsa type dip for tortilla chips)

Dressing

- 1 1/2 tsp. ~ Corn starch
- 1/2 cup ~ Olive oil
- 1/4 cup ~ Red wine vinegar
- 3 Tbsp. ~ Soy sauce
- 1/2 tsp. ~ Coriander seed (ground)
- 1/2 tsp. ~ Cumin (ground)
- 1/2 tsp. ~ Pepper
- 1 clove ~ Garlic (finely minced)
- 1/4 tsp. ~ Garlic salt
- 1/8 tsp. ~ Mustard (powder)
- 4 Tbsp. ~ Honey
- 2 Tbsp. ~ Flax seeds

Salad

- 1 cup ~ Broccoli crowns (diced)
- 1 cup ~ Celery (diced)
- 1 cup ~ Zucchini (diced)
- 1/2 cup ~ Green pepper (diced)
- 1/2 cup ~ Red pepper (diced)
- 1/2 cup ~ Yellow pepper (diced)
- 3 cups ~ Wheat berries
  (precooked ~ pages 16, 18, or 20)
- 1 can [15 oz] ~ Black beans (rinsed)
  (1 1/2 cups)
- 1 cup ~ Tomatoes (fresh ~ diced)

Dressing (make dressing first):

1. Mix corn starch with a little water in a cup until smooth.
2. Place olive oil, vinegar, soy sauce, and seasonings in a small sauce pan and mix well.
3. Cook mixture over medium heat stirring occasionally.
4. After it begins to boil, blend corn starch mixture in with wire whisk.
5. When mixture is a smooth texture and has thickened, remove from heat.
6. Add honey and flax seeds and mix well.
7. Set aside to cool (to room temperature) while salad is being made.

Salad:

1. Dice (in 3/8" pieces) the broccoli, celery, zucchini, green peppers, red peppers, and yellow peppers; place in a large bowl and mix together.
2. Add Wheat Berries, rinsed beans, and tomatoes and mix together.
3. Pour cooled dressing over salad (to taste) and stir in well.
4. Serve at room temperature or cold for a little taste of summer!

Wheat Berry Bean Salad

Yield - 8 cups

Estimated Preparation Time - 15 to 20 minutes

(A new twist to a typical bean salad - it is also a good dip for tortilla chips)

Salad

- 3 cups - Wheat Berries
  (precooked - pages 16, 18, or 20)
- 1 can [15 oz] - Red beans (rinsed)
  (1 1/2 cups)
- 1 can [15 oz] - White beans (rinsed)
  (1 1/2 cups)
- 1 cup - Corn (frozen)
- 1 cup - Green beans (frozen & cut)
- 1/2 cup - Grape tomatoes (sliced)
  (or tomatoes - diced 3/8")
- 1/4 cup - Red onions (diced)
- 4 - Green onions (sliced with greens)
- Red onion rings (1/8" slices)
  (to garnish top of salad)

Dressing

- 1/4 cup - Apple cider vinegar
- 1/4 cup - Honey
- 1/2 tsp. - Pepper
- 1/2 tsp. - Salt
- 2 1/2 Tbsp. - Olive Oil

Salad:

1. Place Wheat Berries in a large mixing bowl.
2. Rinse red and white beans.
3. Cut green beans into 1/2" pieces.
4. Slice grape tomatoes (or dice regular tomatoes - 3/8") and dice red onions.
5. Slice green onions (with greens).
6. Add salad ingredients (except red onion rings) to Wheat Berries and mix together.
7. Pour dressing over salad (to taste) and stir in well.
8. Slice red onion, separate into rings, and garnish the top of the salad.

Dressing:

1. Mix vinegar, honey, salt, and pepper together in a blender.
2. Gradually add olive oil while blending.

∓ Savor the refreshing look and taste of this nutritious salad!

∓ A great dish for those summer picnics.

 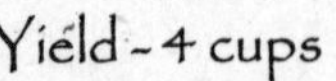

Teriyaki Wheat Lettuce Wraps
Yield ~ 4 cups
Estimated Preparation Time ~ 30 minutes
(A refreshing appetizer or main course)

Sauce
- 2 Tbsp. ~ Soy sauce
- 2 Tbsp. ~ Teriyaki baste & glaze
- 2 Tbsp. ~ Water
- 2 tsp. ~ Corn starch
- 2 tsp. ~ Honey
- 1 tsp. ~ Sesame oil
- 1/4 tsp. ~ Garlic salt
- 1/8 tsp. ~ Pepper

Wraps
- 2 Tbsp. ~ Olive oil
- 4 ~ Green onions (minced)
- 1/2 tsp. ~ Fresh garlic (finely minced)
- 1/2 tsp. ~ Fresh ginger (finely minced)
- 1 can [8 oz] ~ Bamboo shoots (diced)
- 1 can [8 oz] ~ Water chestnuts (diced)
- 1/2 cup ~ Mushrooms (diced)
- 3 cups ~ Wheat Berries (precooked ~ pages 16, 18, or 20)
- 12 ~ Iceberg lettuce "cups" leaves

1. Combine all sauce ingredients in a small bowl, mix well and let sit while preparing other ingredients.
2. Dice (in small pieces) the bamboo shoots, water chestnuts, and mushrooms and set aside.
3. Heat olive oil in a wok or large frying pan over medium high heat. (350° in an electric frying pan)
4. Lightly sauté green onions, garlic, and ginger.
5. Add mushrooms, bamboo shoots, and water chestnuts and stir.
6. Pour sauce over ingredients and mix.
7. Combine Wheat Berries with mixture, stir well, and cook until sauce thickens about 1 to 2 minutes.
8. Serve in lettuce cups (or leaves), roll up, take a bite and savor the moment.

℘ This refreshing appetizer or meal is a dining delight anytime!

Suggestions:
- When using head lettuce, cut in half to separate individual cups (leaves).
- Serve on a bed of cellophane rice noodles (break into small pieces and cook).
- Use celery in place of either bamboo shoots or water chestnuts.

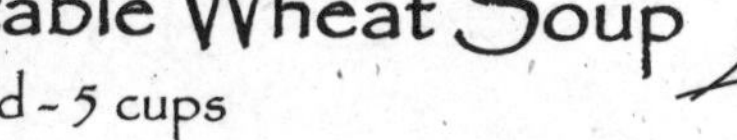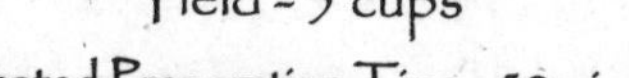

Creamy Vegetable Wheat Soup

Yield ~ 5 cups

Estimated Preparation Time ~ 50 minutes

(A hearty soup to warm up your day ~ great served in a bread bowl)

- 1 Tbsp. ~ Olive oil
- 1/2 cup ~ Onion (diced)
- 2 cloves ~ Garlic (finely minced)
- 2 cups ~ Water
- 1 tsp. ~ Beef (or other) bouillon
  (or equivalent for 1 cup of broth)
- 1 1/4 tsp. ~ Garlic salt
- 1/2 tsp. ~ Pepper
- 1/4 tsp. ~ Ginger (ground)
- 1/8 tsp. ~ Oregano (ground)
- 1 cup ~ Carrots (fresh sliced)
- 1 cup ~ Red potatoes (cubed)
- 1 cup ~ Celery (sliced)
- 1 cup ~ Mushrooms (fresh sliced)
- 2 cups ~ Creamy Wheat Berries
  (precooked ~ pages 17, 19, or 21)

---

1. Cube potatoes (1/2" cubes) and slice carrots, celery, and mushrooms.
2. Heat olive oil in a medium size pan over medium heat.
3. Saute' onions and garlic in the oil until lightly browned.
4. Mix water, bouillon, and seasonings in with the onions and garlic.
5. Increase heat, add carrots and potatoes and bring to a boil.
6. Reduce heat, cover, and simmer (just below boiling) until carrots and potatoes are tender ~ about 30 minutes.
7. Bring to a low boil, stir in celery and mushrooms and cook until celery is tender ~ about 3 to 4 minutes.
8. Mix in Creamy Wheat Berries.
9. Heat to serving temperature, stirring occasionally ~ about 5 to 6 min.
10. This soup is a complete meal that will warm you up from the inside.

વ A pressure cooker can reduce the cooking time of the potatoes and carrots significantly.

Suggestions:
- Use your favorite bouillon flavor instead of beef.
- Experiment with different vegetables.
- Add your favorite meat for a whole new taste.

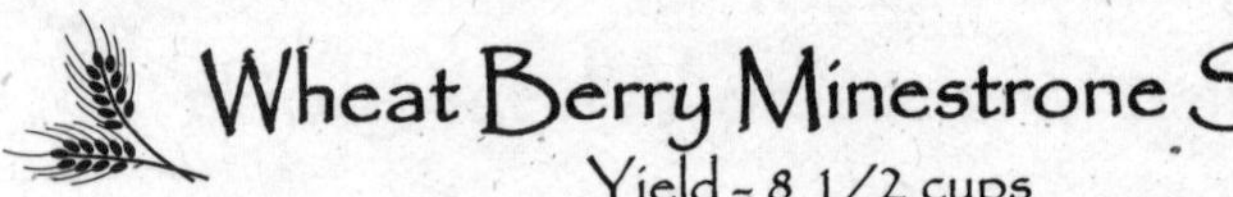

Wheat Berry Minestrone Soup

Yield - 8 1/2 cups

Estimated Preparation Time - 50 minutes

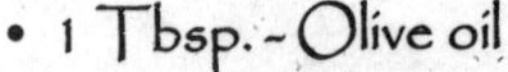

(Enjoy a zesty taste of Italy with this favorite soup)

- 1 Tbsp. - Olive oil
- 1/2 cup - Onion (diced)
- 2 cloves - Garlic (finely minced)
- 2 cups - Water
- 1 tsp. - Tomato bouillon (or equivalent for 1 cup of broth)
- 3 Tbsp. - Spaghetti sauce seasoning (Italian herbs & spices)
- 3/8 tsp. - Pepper
- 1/4 tsp. - Salt

- 1 cup - Carrots (sliced)
- 1 cup - Red potatoes (cubed)
- 1 cup - Mushrooms (fresh sliced)
- 1/2 cup - Celery (sliced)
- 3 cups - Creamy Wheat Berries (precooked - pages 17, 19, or 21)
- 1 can [14.5 oz] - Diced stewed tomatoes with juice (1 1/2 cups)
- 1 can [15 oz] - Red beans (rinsed) (1 1/2 cups)

---

1. Cube potatoes (1/2" cubes) and slice carrots, celery, and mushrooms.
2. Heat olive oil in a large pan over medium heat.
3. Saute onions and garlic in the oil until lightly browned.
4. Mix water, bouillon, and seasonings in with the onions and garlic.
5. Increase heat, add carrots and potatoes and bring to a boil.
6. Reduce heat, cover, and simmer (just below boiling) until carrots and potatoes are tender - <u>about 30 minutes.</u>
7. Bring to a low boil, stir in mushrooms and celery and cook until celery is tender - <u>about 3 to 4 minutes.</u>
8. Mix in Creamy Wheat Berries, tomatoes, and rinsed beans.
9. Heat to serving temperature, stirring occasionally - <u>about 5 to 6 min.</u>
10. Serve hot with fresh grated Romano or Parmesan cheese and bread sticks—"now that's Italian!"

ଓ A pressure cooker can reduce the cooking time of the potatoes and carrots significantly.

<u>Suggestion:</u>
- Serve with a salad and/or your favorite pasta.

Taco Wheat Berry Soup

Yield ~ 8 cups

Estimated Preparation Time ~ 20 to 25 minutes

(A south of the border taste that will make you say ole´!)

- 1 Tbsp. ~ Olive oil
- 3/8 cup ~ Onion (diced)
- 1/2 cup ~ Water
- 1/4 cup ~ Taco seasoning (1.25 oz. package)
- 2 cups ~ Creamy Wheat Berries (precooked ~ pages 17, 19, or 21)
- 1 can [28 oz] ~ Diced stewed tomatoes with juice (3 cups)
- 1 can [15 oz] ~ Kidney beans (rinsed) (1 1/2 cups)
- 1 cup ~ Corn (frozen)
- 1 cup ~ Green beans (frozen & cut)
- 1 can [10.75 oz] ~ Tomato soup
- 1 can [6 oz] ~ Diced green chilies (optional)
- Grated cheese (to taste)
- Sour cream (to taste)

---

1. Heat olive oil in a large pan over medium heat.
2. Saute´ onions in the oil until lightly browned.
3. Mix water and taco seasoning in with the onions.
4. Add Creamy Wheat Berries, mix well, and heat.
5. Increase heat to medium high.
6. Rinse kidney beans, and cut green beans into 1/2" pieces.
7. Add tomatoes, kidney beans, corn, green beans, tomato soup, and green chilies to mixture and stir (add water as needed for desired consistency).
8. Heat to serving temperature, stirring occasionally ~ about 8 to 10 min.
9. Serve this tasty soup with grated cheese, sour cream, and corn or tortilla chips—choose your toppings and enjoy.

ᘓ This soup will spice up your day and bring you back for seconds!

Suggestions:

- Try Wheat Berries (chewier texture) instead of Creamy Wheat Berries.
- Serve in a bread bowl, with corn bread, a tortilla, or crackers.
- Add other grains to your diet by substituting Creamy Multi~Grain Berries (pages 17, 19, or 21) for the Creamy Wheat Berries in this soup.

Wheat Berry Chili

Yield ~ 10 cups

Estimated Preparation Time ~ 25 to 30 minutes

(A great dish to warm up those cold winter days)

- 2 Tbsp. ~ Olive oil
- 1 1/2 ~ Onions (diced)
- 2 cups ~ Water
- 1 ~ Chili brick (20 oz.)
- 4 cups ~ Wheat Berries
  (precooked ~ pages 16, 18, or 20)
- 4 cans [15 oz] ~ Red beans (rinsed)
  (6 cups)
- 1/2 cup ~ Ketchup (optional)
- Chili powder (to taste)
- Pepper (to taste)
- Grated cheese (optional)

---

1. Heat olive oil in a large pan over medium heat.
2. Saute' onions in the oil until lightly browned.
3. Mix chili brick (typically located in the frozen food section) and water in with the onions.
4. Increase heat to medium high.
5. Add Wheat Berries, mix well, and heat.
6. Mix in rinsed beans and ketchup.
7. Stir in chili powder and pepper (to taste).
8. Heat to serving temperature, stirring occasionally ~ <u>about 8 to 10 min.</u>
9. Top with grated cheese (if desired).
10. Serve with your favorite crackers or bread and enjoy!

ଔ This chili will warm you up and keep you going.

Suggestions:

- Precook 2 1/2 cups (1 pound) of dry red beans to use in the chili recipe.
  - Use a pressure cooker to reduce the cooking time for dry beans.
- Replace the chili brick with the following ingredients.
  - 5 tsp. ~ Chili powder
  - 1 1/2 tsp. ~ Cumin
  - 1 tsp. ~ Salt
  - 3/4 tsp. ~ Pepper
  - 1/2 tsp. ~ Paprika

Vegetable Wheat Berries

Yield ~ 6 cups

Estimated Preparation Time ~ 3 minutes

(A quick easy meal for those on the run)

- 3 cups ~ Wheat Berries (chilled) (precooked ~ pages 16, 18, or 20)
- 1 cup ~ Broccoli cuts (frozen)
- 1 cup ~ Carrots (frozen sliced)
- 1 cup ~ Corn (frozen)
- 2 Tbsp. ~ Soy sauce
- 1/4 tsp. ~ Garlic salt
- 1/8 tsp. ~ Pepper

---

1. Place chilled Wheat Berries in a large mixing bowl and stir.
2. Thaw frozen vegetables and mix with the Wheat Berries.
3. Add soy sauce, garlic salt, and pepper and mix well.
4. Serve hot or cold—it is good either way.

∛ In just a few minutes you can create a full meal or a side dish that won't slow you down!

Suggestions:

- Roll in lettuce cups or leaves for a refreshing change.
- Use fresh lightly steamed vegetables in place of frozen.
- Try other types of vegetables.
- Experiment with different types of spices.
- Mix your favorite seasonings and vegetables to make your own creation.
- Enjoy the benefits of other grains by using Multi-Grain Berries (pages 16, 18, or 20) instead of the Wheat Berries in this recipe.

Wheat Berry Stir Fry

Yield ~ 8 cups

Estimated Preparation Time ~ 25 to 30 minutes

(You will love this stir fry which is similar to the familiar Chinese dish "fried rice")

- 2 tsp. ~ Olive oil
- 3 ~ Eggs (scrambled & cut up)
- 1/8 tsp. ~ Pepper
- 2 cups ~ Mushrooms (sliced)
- 1 Tbsp. ~ Butter
- 1/8 tsp. ~ Garlic salt
- 1 cup ~ Broccoli cuts (frozen)
- 1 cup ~ Carrots (frozen sliced)
- 1 cup ~ Corn (frozen)
- 1 cup ~ Green peas (frozen)
- 3 cups ~ Wheat Berries (chilled) (precooked ~ pages 16, 18, or 20)
- 1/2 cup ~ Ham (3/8" cubes) (optional)
- 3 Tbsp. ~ Soy sauce
- Salt & pepper (to taste)

---

1. Heat olive oil in a large frying pan over medium high heat. (350° in an electric frying pan)
2. Scramble eggs in a small bowl, pour into hot oil, and sprinkle with pepper.
3. Cook the eggs until they are firm enough to flip—flip over and cook the other side.
4. Remove cooked eggs (large pancake shape about 1/4" thick) from pan and cut into 1/2" squares.
5. Sauté mushrooms with butter and garlic salt, drain liquid and set aside.
6. Heat frozen vegetables in the preheated frying pan.
7. Add chilled Wheat Berries and mix ingredients together.
8. Combine eggs and drained mushrooms with other ingredients, stir well, and heat mixture evenly.
9. Add <u>precooked</u> ham (if desired) and mix in.
10. Drizzle mixture evenly with soy sauce and stir in.
11. Season with salt, pepper, and additional soy sauce (if desired).
12. Get out the chop sticks and serve this stir fry for lunch or dinner.

ଔ Wheat Berry Stir Fry has become a "real favorite!"

<u>Suggestions:</u>
- Use fresh lightly steamed vegetables in place of frozen.
- Try sautéd green onions and/or other types of vegetables.

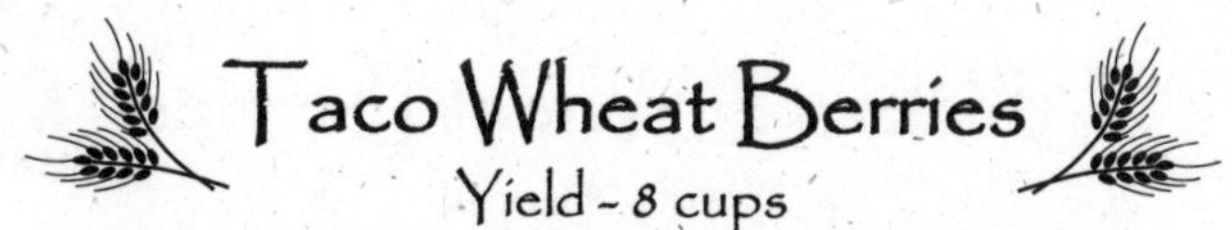

Taco Wheat Berries

Yield ~ 8 cups

Estimated Preparation Time ~ 30 to 40 minutes

(Great served in tacos, lettuce wraps, salads, or as a stand alone dish)

- 1 Tbsp. ~ Olive oil
- 1/2 cup ~ Onion (diced)
- 3/4 cup ~ Water
- 1/4 cup ~ Taco seasoning
    (1.25 oz. package)
- 3 cups ~ Wheat Berries (chilled)
    (precooked ~ pages 16, 18, or 20)
- 1 cup ~ Corn (frozen)

- 1 can [15 oz] ~ Black beans (rinsed)
    (1 1/2 cups)
- 1 cup ~ Green beans (frozen & cut)
- 1/2 cup ~ Black olives (sliced)
- 1 cup ~ Grape tomatoes (sliced)
    (or tomatoes ~ diced 3/8")
- 1/4 tsp. ~ Pepper

---

1. Rinse black beans and cut green beans into 1/2" pieces.
2. Slice olives and grape tomatoes (or dice regular tomatoes ~ 3/8").
3. Heat olive oil in a large frying pan over medium high heat. (350° in an electric frying pan)
4. Sauté onions in the oil until lightly browned.
5. Mix water and taco seasoning in with the onions.
6. Add chilled Wheat Berries and mix together.
7. Combine corn, black beans, green beans, and olives with the other ingredients, stir well, and heat mixture evenly.
8. Mix in tomatoes and sprinkle with pepper (to taste).
9. Serve hot and enjoy this savory south of the border dish with those you love.

ର Get out the chips and liven things up with this dish.

ର Don't be shy, add the finishing touches such as: salsa, guacamole, sour cream and other favorite toppings.

Suggestions:
- Serve with cheese, lettuce, tomatoes, and other taco ingredients.
- Use fresh lightly steamed vegetables in place of frozen.

Chicken & Wheat Berries

Yield ~ 8 cups

Estimated Preparation Time ~ 1 hour 40 minutes

(A welcoming dinner to come home to!)

- 1/4 cup ~ Butter
- 2 ~ Large chicken breasts (boned, skinned, and cut up)
- 4 cups ~ Wheat Berries (precooked ~ pages 16, 18, or 20)
- 1 can [10.75 oz] ~ Cream of chicken soup
- 1 can [10.75 oz] ~ Cream of celery or mushroom soup
- 1 pkg. [1 oz] ~ Onion soup (dry mix)

---

1. Preheat oven to 350°.
2. Cut chicken breasts into 1" cubes.
3. Melt butter in 9" x 13" baking dish to coat the bottom.
4. Mix chicken, Wheat Berries, canned soups, and onion soup mix together in a large bowl.
5. Spread mixture in the baking dish and cook uncovered at 350° until top is golden brown ~ about 1 hour 30 minutes.
6. Relax and enjoy this dish at the end of a long hard day.

ଔ Save room for seconds—you are going to love this one!

Suggestions:

- Add a package [16 oz] of California blend frozen vegetables to the mixture (step 4 above) for a wonderful addition to this tasty dish!
- Serve with your favorite fresh steamed vegetables.
- Try cooking Chicken & Wheat Berries in a slow cooker (Crock Pot).
- Add a whole new dimension to this great dish by using Multi~Grain Berries in place of the Wheat Berries.

Daniel's Pulse
Yield - 12 cups
Estimated Preparation Time - 1 hour 10 minutes
(An interpretation of the Old Testament dish eaten by the prophet Daniel)

- 1 cup - Barley kernels (hulled)
- 1 cup - Chickpeas (dry)
- 1 cup - Rye kernels
- 1 cup - Wheat kernels
- 8 cups - Water

- 1 tsp. - Salt
- 1 tsp. - Cumin (ground)
- 4 cloves - Garlic (finely minced)
- 1/4 tsp. - Garlic salt
- 3/8 tsp. - Pepper

---

1. Place grain, chickpeas, water, and salt in a large pan (5 quarts or more) and stir.
2. Bring mixture to a boil over high heat.
3. Reduce heat, cover and simmer (just below boiling) until done - <u>about 1 hour</u>.
   - Kernels should be chewy with some kernels broken open when done.
   - Mixture should always be wet while cooking.
4. Drain any remaining water and chill mixture.
5. Add cumin, minced garlic (to taste), garlic salt, and pepper to chilled grains and mix together well.
6. Step back in time and experience a dish from the Old Testament (serve hot or cold).

cs Ideally, little or no water should be left over after cooking the grain.

cs A pressure cooker can reduce the cooking time significantly - follow the pressure cooker Multi-Grain Berries recipe on page 20.

cs This pulse recipe is based on an Old Testament study guide which identifies the basic ingredients of pulse as, "such seeds and grains as peas, wheat, barley, and rye". Chickpeas became the pea of choice for a number of reasons: chickpeas are high in protein and were likely used during the time of Daniel (they have been cultivated for thousands of years in the Middle East), in addition, chickpeas cook in about the same length of time as wheat, rye, and barley kernels. The seasonings used in this recipe are also common to the Middle East and could have been used by Daniel.

cs As you savor this unique dish from the past remember Daniel and the benefits he experienced from eating pulse (see Daniel - chapter 1 in the Bible).

Other Grain Berry Uses
Adding Tasty Nutrition to the Things You Eat

The uses for cooked grain berries are virtually unlimited! In addition to the recipes included in this book, a number of other ways to use <u>cooked</u> whole grain kernels are listed below:

Grain Berry Toppings:

- Sprinkle seasoned grain berries on top of salads.
- Garnish a bowl of soup with grain berries (seasoned or unseasoned).
- Crumble a flavored mixture of grain berries on top of desserts or yogurt.
- Dust vegetable dishes with seasoned grain berries.
- Top sandwich fixings with grain berries (seasoned or unseasoned).

Mixing Grain Berries:

- Combine grain berries with oat meal and other hot cereals.
- Mix grain berries into pancake and waffle batter..
- Add grain berries (seasoned or unseasoned) to vegetable dishes.
- Combine grain berries with bread dough and cook (to add a chewy texture).
- Stir grain berries (seasoned or unseasoned) into all types of sauces.
- Mix grain berries (with or without flavoring) with pudding or yogurt.
- Blend grain berries into smoothies, shakes, and malts.
- Include grain berries with your favorite cookie recipe.
- Mix different fruits and/or vegetables with grain berries to create new dishes.

Grain Berry Substitutes:

- Replace part or all of the rice in a recipe with grain berries.
- Substitute different types of grain berries for various hot cereals.
- Use grain berries in spaghetti sauces instead of meat.

The only limitation to expanding your use of grain berries is your imagination. Explore new ways to use them as whole grains become a part of your life!

For additional copies of
Discover Wheat & Other Grains
Visit your favorite store or our website.

www.DiscoverWheat.com

For group presentations please contact us on our website.